MW01284802

Why?

A Layman's Guide to the Liturgy

by

Burnell F. Eckardt, Jr.
Editor-in-Chief, *Gottesdienst*
Evangelical-Lutheran Liturgical Press
Kewanee, Illinois

Repristination Press
Malone, Texas

Text © 1998–2005 by *Gottesdienst*.
Published by Permission.

Repristination Press
716 HCR 3424 E
Malone, TX 76660
hunnius@aol.com

ISBN 1-891469-45-2

The Table of Contents

THE LUTHERAN MASS, BY PARTS

THE INVOCATION

THE CONFESSION OF SINS

THE INTROIT

THE KYRIE

THE GLORIA IN EXCELSIS

THE SALUTATION

THE COLLECT

THE READINGS

THE GRADUAL

THE HALLELUJAH

THE SENTENCE

THE NICENE CREED

THE SERMON

Foreword

Not long ago, historically speaking, most of America was unsettled wilderness. And though refinement and progress have changed the landscape, we Americans still find ourselves only a brief century and a half removed from that wild frontier of precarious settlements repeatedly victimized by cattle rustlers, stagecoach bandits, and revivalists barking up trees. America remains a hard place for faith to flourish, and although today's marauders of the fruited plains now themselves have front lawns and cell phones, they remain in another respect very much like their forebears. They will have nothing to do with icons, vestments, crucifixes, or sacraments. Their churches have no use for an organ, preferring instead the instruments of popular song. Their altars (if they still have them) are covered up but by projector screens for "songs" presented by PowerPoint presentations for all to follow. Their sacraments are shoved aside as relics of a quaint history they now claim to know better than to promote. Their preachers meander through the crowd wearing none of the vestments designating the office they hold. This is America at the dawn of the twenty-first century. It is still the frontier, and it is still wild, especially when it comes to American religion.

Yet there can still be found now and again some remnants and pockets of genuine Christianity, and people who truly appreciate there the Gospel's sublime beauty and dignity. But since they are hemmed in on every side by foreign elements, they find themselves beginning to ask questions about why liturgical things are done the way they are done. *Why do we do things this way? Why is our music so different? Why do we repeat the words of our worship the same way? Why is worship structured the way it is?*

Or again, *Why does the pastor wear that pretty robe?* That was the first such question I ever posed in our parish's newsletter, together with its answer, in an attempt to help the people to understand some of the liturgical customs we have. Soon people began asking their own questions, and so, as a prelude to our Sunday morning adult catechesis, I began to offer a ten-minute period for discussion of some liturgical question or other, a question someone would introduce with the announcement, "I have a Why." *Why do we chant? Why do we kneel? Why do we bow the head?* To this day the practice remains popular here.

Before long many of these questions began to appear in the liturgical journal *Gottesdienst*, of which I became chief editor about ten years ago. Readers soon began to ask permission to print these columns in their newsletters. Now at last, with the help of Fr. James Heiser of Repristination Press, we have put all the Whys together into this booklet. Here you are. We hope this little book will begin to answer at least some basic liturgical questions people have, and so in a small way work toward watering the little remaining oases of liturgy in the wild American wilderness.

I wish to express my sincere appreciation for the gracious offer of publication from Fr. Heiser and his Repristination Press. Thanks also must be accorded to Fr. John Fenton, Chaplain Jonathan Shaw, Dr. Daniel Reuning, and other nameless and distant sources for the provision of seminal material from which I extracted so much of the content herein—though I claim sole responsibility for any errors. In addition, I must acknowledge the tireless efforts of Kathryn Ann Hill, copyeditor, whose brilliant linguistic and theological acumen is as rare as it is precious. As I indicated above, the people of my parish, St. Paul's Evangelical Lutheran Church of Kewanee—especially my wife Carol and our six sons—were integral in promoting the idea of asking these liturgical questions, and I am profoundly in their debt for their constant encouragement. Here, thanks to them, are many such Whys and their answers.

+ *Burnell F. Eckardt Jr.*
The Fifth Sunday of Michaelmas Tide, 2005

GENERAL

Why is Christian worship liturgical?

Liturgical worship is worship according to a set and traditional format drawn from the Sacred Scriptures. The words of the Holy Liturgy are words which have been handed down to us through generations of Christianity. While there are variations in those forms and in which words of liturgy are used where, the basis of Christian liturgy is consistently the use of a standard structure drawn from the wells of Sacred Scripture.

This is, first of all, a safeguard against false worship. For where the Word of God is wanting, there the devil rushes in with his lies. If the structure of Christian worship were left to the whim of the preacher or anyone else, then it would only be a matter of time before those whims would turn away from the sound words of Scripture, since there is nothing good in our flesh. Everything depends on the Word of God. Therefore it is right that our worship be continuously staid upon a sound structure which upholds the Word.

Secondly, liturgical worship is, simply put, using God's own words to speak to God. God gives us His Word, and we speak it back to Him. This is liturgical worship. The Psalms, which have always had a prominent place in the worship of Christians, are both words of God and words of prayer. He gives us the very words with which to pray to Him. Liturgical worship is the employment of these words. We pray using the words He has given us to pray, and in this way we rejoice in them.

Third, liturgical worship is giving honor where honor is due. The Church of all times has worshiped in this manner. When we do the same we show our respect for the Christian tradition of all times, and we worship indeed with angels and archangels and all the company of heaven. ✠

Why do we worship on Sunday?

Actually, in apostolic times, the Church was at prayer together daily, according to Acts 2: They continued steadfastly in the apostles' doctrine and fellowship: the breaking of the bread and the prayers. Even so, they reserved Sunday for the high feast, inasmuch as they recognized Sunday, the first day of the week, as the day when Christ arose from the dead. The Sabbath had been Saturday, of course, but this was fulfilled when Christ rested in the tomb on Holy Saturday. This is why the

Apostle declares that Sabbaths are a shadow of things to come, but the substance is of Christ. So therefore Sunday became the Church's "high" day of worship, since Christ Himself not only arose on Sunday, but made His subsequent resurrected appearances also on Sundays throughout the forty days leading to His ascension. Then came Pentecost, the fiftieth day from Easter, also a Sunday. So it was Christ Himself who shifted the thinking of His people toward Sunday as the chief of days. Moreover, since, according to St. Luke's Gospel, He was recognized by the Emmaus disciples (on Sunday) in the breaking of the bread, and that phrase is repeated in Acts (see above), so it was fitting that Sunday be also the chief day on which the Holy Sacrament was offered to the people.

So it was, throughout the ages, that Holy Christendom, whether or not they assembled also on other days of the week, would always assemble every Sunday (which, biblically, begins on Saturday night), in order especially to receive the Holy Sacrament in the Mass.

Therefore the orders of Matins and Vespers, as well as other non-Communion services, were really never intended as replacements for the Mass on Sunday morning. Rather, they were used either on weekdays or as pre-sacramental services. But Sunday was reserved especially for high worship, that is, for the reception of the Holy Supper. ✠

Why is Holy Communion sometimes called Mass?

There are actually many different names for the service of the Holy Sacrament. It is called the Eucharist, the Holy Supper, the Holy Communion, the Lord's Supper, the Sacrament of the Altar, and the Mass. In the New Testament and early church times is was called the Breaking of the Bread.

The term Mass (Latin, *missa*) is perhaps the term with most widespread use throughout Christendom. It is also a source of controversy among Protestants because of its regular association with Roman Catholicism. The Lutheran Reformation renounced the Roman Mass as "the greatest and most horrible abomination, as it directly and powerfully conflicts with this chief article [of justification by faith in Christ]" (Smalcald Articles II, 1). Yet the context of this statement will determine what it is that is abominable about the Roman Mass, for Luther's quote continues: "... it has been held that this sacrifice or work of the Mass, even though it be rendered by a wicked scoundrel, frees men from sins, both in this life and also in purgatory, while only the Lamb of God shall and must do this" (ibid.). Thus it is clear that what Luther opposed was the Roman idea of Mass as an act or work of man, essentially of re-sacrificing the body of Christ for sins. For Rome the benefits of the Mass were effected by the work that the priest performed. For Luther and the Lutherans, the benefit was seen in the words, "Given and shed for you for the remission of sins." Thus in the Mass the Sacrament was to be received orally by the communicants in order for them to benefit from it.

Yet the term Mass was never abandoned on the Lutheran side. Indeed the Lutheran Confessions declare,

> We do not abolish the Mass but religiously keep and defend it. In our churches Mass is celebrated every Sunday and on other festivals, when the sacrament is offered to those who wish for it after they have been examined and absolved. We keep traditional liturgical forms, such as the order of the lessons, prayers, vestments, etc. (Apology to the Augsburg Confession XXIV, 1)

In America, the term has been looked on with suspicion among many Lutherans, which is likely due to a long-held bias against anything "Catholic." This bias is unfortunate especially because it leads to the preference of tendencies and terms which are in much more abundant use among churches which deny altogether the real presence of Christ in the Sacrament. Dr. C. F. W. Walther, founding father of the Missouri Synod, had this to say about such a bias: "It is a pity and dreadful cowardice when a person sacrifices the good ancient church customs to please the deluded American sects, lest they accuse one of being papistic!" (*Essays for the Church* [St. Louis: Concordia Publishing House, 1992], 1:194.)

Since we agree that the Sacrament is truly the Body and Blood of Christ—a point of agreement with Rome, and of disagreement with Methodists, Baptists, and others—and since historically, confessing Lutherans have not shunned the use of the term Mass, therefore we ought not be ashamed to use it, if only to distinguish ourselves from anyone who would deny that the bread is truly Christ's Body, and the wine is truly His Blood. ✠

Why do we dress well for church?

Sometimes it is said that people dress up for church only to show off. This is both improper to think (for we are required by the Eighth Commandment to think well and not evil of our neighbors) and likely to be wrong. The Christian's desire to dress appropriately for worship comes from a knowledge of the fact that we come to stand in the presence of God when in church. That is, Christ is present in the Gospel and in the Sacrament. The preaching of the Gospel and the Holy Liturgy contain Christ Himself, and this can be even more profoundly seen in the Holy Sacrament, which is the Body and Blood of Christ. One way to express our faith in this truth is to dress ourselves well, as people who know and live according to this truth. We dress up our building, we dress up our pastor, we dress up our altar and other church furniture. Is it not fitting, then, that we also dress up ourselves, according to our ability?

There is a custom in many churches to dress up a bit more for Sunday than when one attends on another day of the week. This custom has the effect of dressing up the Sunday itself a little more in recognition of our Lord's resurrection on a Sunday.

It is fitting to talk in general terms about the appropriateness of certain clothing at the altar, since we regard it as sacred space.

But is this a law? Certainly not! It is, rather, by a recognition of the Gospel that we learn to dress ourselves well for church. Christians are freed from the demands of the law in Christ. We live by faith in Him, and our faith has opportunity to express itself according to the freedom of the Gospel.

The law of love does have bearing on this matter, however, in two ways.

First, in that we ought not to become our neighbors' judges, ready to condemn someone for dressing a certain way; we Christians ought to bear with one another's weaknesses, and so fulfill the law of Christ, as the Apostle says. Further, what a poor man might call dressing well ought never be looked upon with scorn by someone who has more than he. For to dishonor the poor is to dishonor Christ.

Second, we ought seek not to give offense by the clothing we wear to the altar, for love of the family of faith ought to be evident especially as we commune together. The liberty of a Christian must always be weighed against the Christian's mindfulness of his neighbor. ✠

Why do we follow liturgical rubrics when some find them offensive?

Such a small thing is the sign of the holy cross, one wonders why anyone should be so stubborn as to continue to make that sign when so many find it so offensive. So also, why should the matter of how we hold our hands when praying be something over which we have to be so unbending? Or yet again, why does a pastor continue to dress in clerical garb every day, when some find even that offensive? There are numerous matters like these which could flesh out the list, matters which appear quite unworthy of such an unyielding comportment on our part: how we vest, how we sing, the kinds of words we speak, etc. Matters such as these lead the uninformed to ask why we are so stubborn, and hence lead also others to insist that we quit being so bullheaded about them. These are matters of *adiaphora* (unessential things), are they not? Yet these are the matters which win for some of us the charges of being unyielding, unbending, and unwilling to work with people.

Why do we insist on these things when we could just as well preach the same Gospel without crossing ourselves all the time, without holding our hands palm to palm, without dressing every day as if we were off to church? Nay, we could do it better, some would allege, for we would not have to contend with controversy over unessential matters; why, these things are lower in rank even than what our dogmatics books would call secondary non-fundamental articles! Surely we could yield here, could we not?

When confessional instincts drive us, we sometimes cannot exactly come up with the answer all at once. After all, there is no false doctrine in not making the sign, or in not praying thus and so, or in dressing in suit and tie for work-a-day pastoral duties.

But that should lead no one to suppose there is no good answer. What may be said first of all about this kind of stubbornness is that it is not likely just for the sake of some personal quirk on our part that we get stoic about some things others would cast into the not-worth-it category. Gilbert Meilaender put the matter quite well once in an issue of *First Things*:

> It cannot be simply my personal view, my personal cause. For that alone I would scarcely risk or endure isolation. Few "opinions" of mine are likely to mean as much to me as my good name among colleagues. So if it is my cause that is at stake, that good name is likely to trump other considerations. No, the truth we think we understand must have about it an impersonality; it cannot simply be one's own private view or opinion. (First Things 47 [November 1994]: 34)

There is another very good reason for this inclination to retain certain practices even if some will find them offensive. David's prayers give the reason: "Zeal for Thy house hath consumed me" (Ps. 69:9); "my zeal hath consumed me" (Ps. 119:139). So also we see Jesus, who for this zeal drove the moneychangers and their oxen and sheep and doves all out of the temple, poured out their money, and overthrew their tables. "Then His disciples remembered that it was written, 'Zeal for Your house has eaten Me up'" (St. John 2:17). Now one could as well say the same of Jesus' behavior as many have said about the behavior of certain confessing Christian pastors. Jesus did not have to pour out their money and overturn their tables. Certainly that was a matter of *adiaphora*. He could as well have complained to the officials, or incited the people; He could have used other means which would have imperiled His own fame far less than this. Why did He do that? The answer is zeal for God's house. This is exactly the reason we confessing pastors are counted stubborn over some of the things we do. They all pertain to worship, they all pertain to the liturgy, and most especially to the blessed Sacraments. The holy sign exalts Baptism and invites the Sacrament of the Altar. The "praying hands" (which many have as statues on their shelves but never praying in that posture, palm to palm, on the ends of their own arms!) portray the serenity of faith staid on the one thing needful, that toward which the one praying faces, that which is upon the altar. The clerical garb calls daily attention to the office which is pre-eminently carried out in the place where such garb is especially called for. These matters are matters of faith, and of zeal. One thing is needful; hearts of faithful preachers (and people), staid on that one thing, will tend not to notice, and certainly not to heed, the gainsayers and their railing. For it is not that they have made some determination to be stubborn about unnecessary things, nor to portray some sort of criticism toward others who don't do it that way; rather, it is simply that zeal has eaten them up. They could not turn back; faith made them do it; truth made them do it; their minds and their bodies are captive to the Word of God. ✠

Why is it important for Christians to receive the Holy Sacrament frequently?

Let's let Martin Luther answer this, from the "Christian Questions with Their Answers" in the Small Catechism: "In respect to God, both the command and the promise of Christ the Lord should move him, and in respect to himself, the trouble that lies heavy on him, on account of which such command, encouragement, and promise are given."

And then Luther continues, "But what shall a person do if he be not sensible of such trouble, and feel no hunger and thirst for the Sacrament?":

> To such a person no better advice can be given than that, in the first place, he put his hand into his bosom, and feel whether he still have flesh and blood, and that he by all means believe what the Scriptures say of it, in Gal. 5 and Rom. 7.

> Secondly, that he look around to see whether he is still in the world, and keep in mind that there will be no lack of sin and trouble, as the Scriptures say, in John 15 and 16; 1 John 2 and 5.

> Thirdly, he will certainly have the devil also about him, who with his lying and murdering, day and night, will let him have no peace within or without, as the Scriptures picture him, in John 8 and 16; 1 Pet. 5; Eph. 6; 2 Tim. 2. ✠

THE SETTING

Why is there an eternal light in the sanctuary?

The eternal light is the candle that hangs from the ceiling of the chancel, on the Gospel side. It is always lit. According to ancient custom, the eternal light signifies not only the light of Christ, as does any candle in the church, but also the fact that there are somewhere in its proximity the reserved elements of the Holy Sacrament. These are called *reliquae*, the fragments that remain (St. Matt. 14:20) following the celebration of the Sacrament. These are set aside for use when the pastor visits the sick and shut-ins. What remains of these by the next Mass are used therein. Yet they are kept separate from what has not yet been consecrated, until after the Words of Institution have been spoken. This is in accord with the maxim of Acts 10:15: "What God has cleansed you must not call common." ✠

Why is church music so different from all other kinds of music?

The music of the Church's liturgy is very ancient in character, but that is not the chief reason it is so different. Rather, it is that the life of the Church is also very different from the life of this world. So the chanting of the words of the liturgy provides an instinctive awareness that here something is taking place which we do not find anywhere in the world. This is a different world, the world of faith and the Holy Ghost. Actually this way of singing, a way foreign to the ways of this world, arises out of the very Word of God. For the parts of the liturgy which we sing are generally portions of psalms. Most of the psalms came from King David, and David himself sang them when they first came forth. How did they sound when he sang them? We don't exactly know, of course, but we do know that when St. Gregory the Great, in about the year A.D. 600, arranged for the compiling of the ancient psalm tones, he compiled the materials already well established in use, which had been taken over from the old synagogue. Thus the Gregorian psalm tones were based on earlier tones, and therefore it is quite likely that the way in which we chant the liturgy today, if it is Gregorian in style, sounds very similar to the way the words sounded when David first uttered them (except for the fact that he sang in Hebrew). Therefore the music of the liturgy does indeed come from another world: the world of the ancients, the world of David, the world of Christ, the world of the kingdom of heaven. ✠

Why does the church have stained-glass windows?

M uch of what passes for "stained glass" these days is actually painted glass, but it generally provides a similar effect, which is threefold. First, it provides an image to look at in a window, something on which to feast the eyes while in church. This is a good thing, because there ought to be plenty of things to look at while at worship. A church which has little or nothing to look at is not taking advantage of one of the two most prominent senses God has given us. St. Paul encourages attention to things of beauty: "Whatsoever things are lovely . . . think on these things" (Phil. 4:8). To fill the eyes with beautiful things at worship is to remind the faithful of the temple whose gate was called "Beautiful" (Acts 3:2), and that in turn reminds them that God Himself is the author of beauty. Moreover, this sense of beauty serves to remind the faithful of the beauty of the incarnation of God. Christ has become flesh, and so has adorned the earth with His own eternal beauty. Should we not therefore attend to what is beautiful?

Secondly, the images portrayed in stained-glass windows are generally images from the Gospel, and thus the maxim comes to mind: "A picture is worth a thousand words." To see an image of Jesus the Good Shepherd, or of Jesus healing someone, or of the resurrected Christ hailing Mary is to bring immediately to mind the most precious truths which give rise to these images; and so the Word of God, as pondered in the heart, has good effect.

Third, the use of light filtered through colored glass provides an effect which is very uncommon anywhere else in the world. Churches still have pretty much of a corner on the market for stained-glass windows, and so the message stands out—a message unspoken yet unmistakable—that this place is unlike any other place in the world. This is where heaven and earth meet (through Christ who is preached and administered here), where He who is the light of the world is shed abroad in our hearts. How fitting, then, that as sunlight is filtered through those windows, so the almighty God is "filtered" to us through His gracious word of life. ✠

Why do churches have arches and pointed ceilings?

Churches with arches which ascend to a point at the top are generally called *Gothic* or *neo-gothic*. In some Gothic churches, if you stand at the entrance and look down the aisle toward the altar, you can see the ribs in the wall that accentuate these arches, architectural lines that move vertically from the bottom of the ceiling vault to the very top. These ribs seem to fit inside one another as one looks down the aisle, as each successive rib is a little farther away from the one before it, and hence, smaller in appearance. The view is, as it were, of a picture frame within a picture frame within a picture frame, from the first to the last rib. What this suggests to the viewer is a sense of looking into another realm altogether.

At the heart of these successive ribs stands the altar, from which Christ's Body and Blood are distributed to His people. Therefore the altar is truly a meeting place between one realm and another, that is, between heaven and earth. When Christ's people receive Christ's Body and Blood, they receive the holy mystery of Christ, divinity contained within humanity, under the holy elements. At the altar we meet heaven; we meet Christ Himself. Truly then, the meeting place of heaven and earth is here; it is fitting, then, that the Gothic structure be employed to help accentuate this mystery and reality. ✠

Why are the flags in the auditorium, not in the church?

According to the American pledge of allegiance, the flag stands for the republic itself. This is why it is proper for Americans to honor the flag, for the republic is due honor as a nation "under God." All nations are "under God," in that they only exist as nations by God's leave, and also in that their authorities are all "ordained of God" (Rom. 13:1). In America, we accord honor to the flag not only because of this, but also because we recognize the value of America's freedoms, which are a gift of God. Thus it is right for Christians to observe proper flag etiquette: to stand when the flag passes at a parade; to display the flag only during daylight or when lighted; to replace any torn or tattered flag; never to wear a flag as an article of clothing, etc.

It is not in the best of Christian tradition, however, to display the national flag in the setting of Christian worship, nor does such a custom have its roots in church history. The history of displaying national flags in churches is of recent origin, and while perhaps well meant, cannot be defended by reference to the universal history of the Church.

Proper flag etiquette does not establish or require the display of the flag in civilian churches. American flag etiquette requires that the American flag take symbolical precedence wherever it is displayed. On a flagpole, it must fly higher than any other flag; on a stage, it must stand at the stage's right hand, the position of honor, called "the flag's own right." So it is arguable that in a church's worship space, where the flag's symbolism *cannot* take precedence over the displayed signs and symbols of the faith (crosses, statues, etc.), it would be better not to display it at all. (Military settings where chaplains serve might legitimately be seen as an exception to this rule, inasmuch as they are themselves government institutions, and the display of the flag in such a context might well be understood as a necessary designation of the government they represent.)

The Church must be completely blind to racial and ethnic origin, since God is not a respecter of persons (Acts 10:34). This also means that if someone from another country should visit us, we would not do well to indicate to that person that we are an *American* church; no, we would rather say that we are a *Christian* church, and you are welcome, whether you are American or not. Christian worship is really not to be identified as an "American" thing. It belongs to all the people of God of all times and places. So it is in the best of Christian tradition to understand the area of worship as something not belonging to any particular nation.

On the other hand, auditoriums across the land really ought to display an American flag. Since the auditorium is not the place of worship, but the place of common assemblies for various purposes, it is therefore proper to designate it as an American place. Here is where the flag truly belongs; an auditorium without a flag is really less than fully furnished. To plant the flag there gives the flag its due honor. ✠

SEASONAL COLORS

Why is violet the color of Advent and Lent?

Violet is the color of royalty, having once been a rare and costly color to which only the rich and royal had access. The rich man who failed to notice poor Lazarus (St. Luke 16:19–31) was "clothed in purple and fine linen." Jesus was clothed in a purple robe when His royalty was mocked by Pilate's soldiers (St. John 19:2).

Therefore it is fitting that the Church employ violet in her seasons of penitence, for our recollection of the scorn heaped upon our Lord must produce contrite hearts. The color of violet therefore serves to symbolize both the true royalty of Christ (the Anointed, cf. Ps. 2) and His humiliation, which ought to humble us all in due preparation to receive Him. Violet is a penitential color, not a festive color. Its rich hue designates somber penitence and prayer. ✠

Why is blue sometimes seen in churches?

The color blue has in recent years been used as an alternate color for Advent, inasmuch as blue universally symbolizes hope. During Advent the Church emphasizes her perpetually hopeful wait for the coming of Christ.

This innovation, while providing a helpful distinction between Advent and Lent, also de-emphasizes the need for understanding Advent as a penitential season. Preparation for the coming of Christ must always be penitential. Moreover, the use of blue for Advent is a departure from its traditional use as the color for the Blessed Virgin Mary. In iconography she has traditionally been seen in red or royal blue, or both, perhaps because she herself is emblematic of the Church's hopeful expectation of the coming of her Son.

The church which has blue paraments might well employ them for the Marian feasts (the Annunciation, March 25, the Visitation, July 2 [or May 31], and the Dormition, August 15), and retain violet for Advent. ✠

Why is the color rose sometimes used liturgically?

The color rose, when it is used, is only seen during two days of the year, Sundays set in the midst of the year's two penitential seasons. Rose is accordingly appropriate for the Third Sunday of Advent (*Gaudete*) and for the Fourth Sunday in Lent (*Laetare*). The reason for this usage is that rose is a lightening of the purple hue, and as such a reminder that even in the depths of sorrows or penitence, Christian faith is appropriately joyful, ever mindful of the victory which Christ has obtained for us. These two Sundays are therefore set at the midpoint of the penitential seasons, and the color rose is employed only on the Sundays themselves, and not for the weeks following them.

Similarly flowers, which are traditionally absent during Lent, are used on *Laetare* Sunday, as a further reminder of the joy set in the midst of penitential sorrows. ✠

Why is black sometimes used liturgically?

The color black is actually the absence of color, and thus has been used to signify a time of somber reflection and deepest sorrow. Recent traditions have employed it for Ash Wednesday, Good Friday, and for any Day of Humiliation and Prayer (appropriate in special circumstances such as the onset of a plague or warfare).

Some traditions which observe so-called Offices of the Dead and Requiem Masses also use black for these.

According to widespread tradition it is violet, the color for Lenten sorrows, which is rather to be used for Ash Wednesday as the first day of Lent, and for a Day of Humiliation and Prayer, as for a day of penitential supplications. On Good Friday, it is also traditional to leave the altar bare, following its stripping after the Maundy Thursday celebration of the Sacrament. This tradition would still employ black for the veiling of crosses and images on Good Friday.

Moreover black, as signifying dignity, is the traditional color for the regular clothing of pastors, as well as for the tippet, a long stole-like scarf worn over cassock and surplice to signify the preaching office, especially when the pastor preaches a sermon at times such as Matins and Vespers, when the Sacrament is not offered. ✠

Why is white the color of Christmas, Epiphany, and Easter?

White is the purest of colors, and therefore the most glorious of colors. It is fitting, therefore, that the color white be used for the feasts of our Lord. Even Pentecost, whose color is red (for the Holy Spirit), was once known as *White-Sunday*, from which the traditional term *Whitsunday* comes. Feast days of saints who were not martyred, such as St. John and St. Mary Magdalene, also employ white, signifying the purity of sainthood.

The seasons of Christmas, Epiphany, and Easter are most appropriately adorned in white, for they commemorate the incarnation and the resurrection of our Lord, which are the greatest of all commemorations. These first-class feasts are also feasts of our Lord, who is Himself the spotless Lamb of God who takes away the sin of the world. In Isaiah, the declaration of God is, "Though your sins are like scarlet, they shall be as white as snow; though they are red like crimson, they shall be as wool" (1:18). The purity of Christ, therefore, is also to be understood as the purity which becomes ours through faith in Him. For He by His merit and sacrifice has obtained for us this purity which is His own, and He gives this purity to us by the proclamation and distribution of the forgiveness of sins through His name. In this way, we become pure and white as He is. Thus it is right to adorn the feasts of Him who is our Lord with white, for they indicate not only His purity, but the purity which belongs by faith to His own faithful flock, received by the means of salvation offered and given in the feast of salvation, the Mass. ✠

Why is red the color of Pentecost?

Red is, of course, the color of fire, which makes it on Pentecost the color of the Holy Spirit's fire resting on the apostles' heads. Red is also used, however, to commemorate any saints who were martyred, for red is the color of blood. This too is related closely to Pentecost, a connection which is often missed. The Pentecostal fire of the Spirit was a token of things to come: these apostles were about to be persecuted severely for preaching the Gospel. Eleven of the Twelve would be martyred for it, and the twelfth, St. John, would be exiled. The Holy Spirit is manifested in the preaching of the Gospel, and a regular result of this manifestation is the same result as occurred in Christ's own ministry. See what happened to Him who said, "The words that I speak to you are spirit, and they are life" (St. John 6:63). Behold, He was crucified. Thus there is a repetition of His life seen in the life of faith:

when the Christian faith is boldly confessed in the world, there Christians take up their crosses and follow Him, as He said. Small wonder, then, that they have been persecuted, hounded, reproached, and martyred. Small wonder, too, that the color of Pentecost is red. ✠

Why is green the color of the second half of the church year?

The color green is the color of life and growth, as foliage reappears in the springtime and remains throughout the summer. Therefore it is fitting that green be used for the second half of the church year, the period following Pentecost and Trinity (Pentecost and the Trinity octave use red and white, respectively) until the end of the church year.

This period is appropriately subdivided into Trinitytide (from Trinity Sunday), St. John's Tide (from the Nativity of St. John the Baptist, June 24), St. Laurence Tide (from St. Laurence Day, August 10), Michaelmas Tide (from Michaelmas, September 29), and All Saints' Tide, also called the Last Sundays of the Church Year (from All Saints' Day, November 1). These subdivisions also serve to emphasize the various stages of the Christian pilgrimage, even as summer itself has various stages.

Traditionally this period has been referred to as *ordinary time*, as opposed to the festival time of the church year which observes particular aspects of the mystery of Christ. Ordinary time therefore refers to the period of time for observing the mysteries of Christ in all their aspects, but none in particular. Perhaps for this reason, there is wide traditional precedent for counting the Sundays after Epiphany and the Baptism of Our Lord as belonging to ordinary time as well. However, the unity of the Epiphany theme throughout the entire period, the theme of the manifestation of the Lord's glory, would suggest the use of white throughout that season, employing green only during summertime, as nature itself also suggests. ✠

PRE-SERVICE

Why are the candles lit from top to bottom and extinguished from bottom to top?

When the candles are lit for the Mass, the ones closest to the center are lit first, moving outward from there. This is to signify that the source of our life and salvation comes from the altar. The altar not only signifies the sacrifice of Christ for our sins, but is also the place from which the Holy Sacrament is given. Christ, the light of the world, is truly given to us, in the Holy Sacrament, from the altar. Therefore the light of the world truly shines forth from the altar. The lighting of candles outward from the altar (the topmost candle being also the innermost candle, and so forth) signifies this truth. Light goes forth from the altar. At the close of the service, the candles are extinguished in reverse order, as a further signification of this: the light returns to the altar whence it came, that we might be reminded that it will come forth from there again and again, to the end of the world. ✠

Why is the cross carried in procession?

When the processional crucifix is carried through the nave to its place in the sanctuary, it leads the way: for the choir, for the attendants, for the clergy, for the celebrant, and indeed, for all the people. Although the people do not actually process (except on Palm Sunday and at the Great Vigil of Easter), they with heart and mind join the procession, being led by the cross. This is to express with our actions our agreement with the words of the apostle Paul, "I determined not to know anything among you except Jesus Christ and Him crucified."

Therefore the proper response of faith to the entrance of the cross is to turn sideways to face it as it passes one's pew on its entrance, and to turn toward the altar as the procession passes. It is also proper even to bow the head and make the sign of the cross at the moment when the cross passes, as a gesture of humility toward the Crucified One. At the close of the Mass, when the cross processes out, it is also fitting to reverence. (It is not necessary to continue facing the cross as it continues all the way to the back of the church, however, as this would involve the unseemly turning of one's back on the Body and Blood of Christ.)

Reverence toward the crucifix is a way of acknowledging Christ's deep humility, saying in effect, if He would so humble Himself, should not I also humble myself? ✠

Why are torches sometimes carried in procession?

The use of torches (i.e., candles on poles) contributes to the beauty and ceremony of a procession. Two torches are carried side by side in procession behind the processional crucifix. As lights on poles, they call to mind the words of Christ concerning light. In one place He says, "I am the light of the world," and in another, to His disciples, "You are the light of the world. A city that is set on a hill cannot be hidden. Nor do they light a lamp and put it under a basket, but on a lampstand, and it gives light to all who are in the house. Let your light so shine before men, that they may see your good works and glorify your Father in heaven." In these words, Christ teaches us that the shining of Christian light is in truth the shining of Christ Himself. When the Christian Church believes, teaches, and confesses the Gospel, the light which is Christ Himself shines. Since in the Mass Christ is preached and confessed, therefore it is fitting that candles be employed; and so too, to add to the celebration, candles on poles, or torches. ✠

THE LUTHERAN MASS, GENERAL

Why does the pastor only wear that pretty robe some of the time?

That pretty robe is called a *chasuble*, and it is a special vestment to be worn by the celebrant at Holy Communion. The reason for vestments at all is primarily to remind both the pastor and his people that he is not performing his "own thing" during the Mass, but is standing in for Christ, that is, serving as Christ's ambassador for the people. Another way to think of this is to consider the sacred paintings that arose out of the early church, called *icons*. An icon was used to focus a person's attention on the holy matters of the faith by what was pictured—in most cases, Christ Himself. So when one looked at the icon, one could adore and ponder the holy Christ Himself who, as it were, stood *behind* the icon. A good way to think of the pastor, especially when he is celebrating the Lord's Supper, is to think of him as an icon: in this case, a living icon. Behind him stands Christ, or rather, in him. He serves as Christ, saying, "This is my body," etc. Thus it is very helpful for the pastor, when he is attentive to this most important matter of celebrating the Sacrament, to be wearing the chasuble, in order visually to remind the people and himself that here especially he is standing in for Christ, serving as Christ to the people.

But he only wears it for that, in order to emphasize the special character of the Mass. The Sacrament and all things pertaining to it should be dressed in their finest attire, to make our faith most clear: *this* is the heart of our faith, worship, and life. So, in other prayer offices, such as Matins, though he will vest, yet he will not wear the chasuble, reserving the latter only for the Sacrament. ✠

Why do we stand up for the last stanza of some hymns?

A good number of our hymns have as a last stanza a *Trinitarian doxology*. This is an ascription of praise to the Holy Trinity. Doxology comes from two Greek words: *doxa*, which means "praise," and *logia*, which means "words," hence, "praise words." A Trinitarian doxology is therefore simply an ascription of praise to Father, Son, and Holy Spirit (Holy Ghost). This is a custom dating to the early church, when the psalms were sung with a Gloria Patri at their conclusion (as we still do when we sing psalms). The Gloria Patri (Latin for "Glory be to the Father," its opening words) is itself the earliest form of the Trinitarian doxology, and was added to the psalms to indicate that these Old Testament prayers have now been fulfilled in Christ our Lord, who commanded Baptism in the name of the Father and of the Son and of the Holy Ghost. When Christian hymns began to be written, they were generally seen as psalms in verse, and hence the Gloria easily found its way into their last stanza. Since the Psalmist declares that it is by His name that God saves us (e.g., Ps. 54), it is good and fitting for Christian people, according to long-standing custom, to honor the blessed name of the Holy Trinity whenever it is expressed aloud. Indeed, not only standing but also the bowing of the head is appropriate at the point when the name Father, Son, and Holy Ghost is sung. Some churches even have the custom of making the sign of the cross at this point. Such bodily involvement in the liturgy is always helpful, as an indication that in Christ our whole body, mind, and soul are held captive to the Word of God. ✠

Why do we "fold our hands" for prayer?

The folding of hands is, traditionally, the placing of hands palm to palm (as opposed to the interlocking of fingers). The celebrant and attendants at the Mass hold their hands this way whenever their hands are not otherwise occupied. People at prayer or approaching the altar may also fittingly have hands folded palm to palm.

To fold the hands palm to palm might well be considered the liturgical "clapping" of the hands, as it is written in Psalm 47, "Oh, clap your hands, all you peoples!" As everything is to be done decently and in order, as the Apostle also says, we do not indiscriminately clap our hands, as if to applaud, in the service. Such "clapping" is in our culture meant for showing appreciation or praise for someone. But since the Mass is not from our culture, but rather has, as it were, a culture of its own, a heavenly culture, as it were, we do not customarily employ cultural expressions of praise in church. So we would not "clap" for God (nor certainly for anyone else) in the way that we clap at a concert. Rather, the Mass calls for a different kind of "clapping," one of profound reverence, which does not make noise or indiscriminate movement. The liturgical equivalent of such "clapping" is, simply, the folding of the hands palm to palm. Such "clapping" is always directed toward God.

More significantly, hands held palm to palm are manifestly not *working* hands; they are *resting* hands, hands which are not doing anything. This is an expression of faith, then, that we trust not in our own works or accomplishments, but rest in the works which Christ has accomplished for us. As the hymn writer has said it, "Nothing in my hand I bring; simply to Thy cross I cling." So then, empty hands, hands not at work, are held palm to palm, as if to say without words, I rest in the works of Christ; He has said to me, "It is finished," and therefore I am confident in my prayers that God will hear me without my doing or earning anything at all. All has been earned; all has been done! This I believe, and I boast in the works of Christ alone; therefore when at prayer I will gladly fold my hands to show that these hands would not wish to obscure the work of Christ; far be it from these hands to attempt to make God hear me; rather, I know that He will hear me for His own name's sake; for His name is Father, Son, and Holy Spirit; and this name was given to me in Baptism. Therefore I will follow the psalm which says, "Be still and know that I am God." ✠

Why do the people say or sing "Amen" at various places in the Mass?

The word *Amen* is a Hebrew word whose meaning carried over also into Greek, which simply means "truly." Whenever Jesus' words, for example, are translated "Truly, truly I say to you," what is actually found in the Greek original are the words "*Amen, amen lego hymin.*" This is why the Catechism tells us that what is meant by *Amen* is "Yes, yes, it shall be so," or, "This is most certainly true." For the word in Christian usage is a great emphatic word of confession of the Faith, as it has long been so, dating from the days of Moses. Moses instructed that the people were at various times to say their *Amen*, and from thenceforth the people of Israel did so instinctively. So when the Levites brought the ark of God and set it in the midst of the tent David had pitched for it, the Levites sang a song of praise recorded in 1 Chronicles 16. When they finished singing, "all the people said, 'Amen!' and praised the Lord." So also, the Psalms are filled with *Amens* amid songs of praise. In the early church, according to St. Paul (1 Cor. 14:16) it was customary for the people to say "Amen" at the giving of thanks, undoubtedly because the church's form of prayer and Mass followed the patterns set long before in the synagogue by the Sacred Scriptures.

There is really no more concise and emphatic a Christian confession than "Amen." This is why it is most appropriate for Christian people to be accustomed to saying this word from the heart at set times during the Mass. The times for *Amens* are not spontaneous, however, but are according to set rubrics, in order to preserve good order and propriety in worship, as the Apostle instructs the church, saying, "The spirits of the prophets are subject to the prophets," and again, "Let all things be done decently and in order" (1 Cor. 14:32, 40). So "Amen" is appropriately said whenever the pastor blesses the people, whenever the Trinitarian name is invoked, or even at the altar, when the Sacrament is given and received. ✠

Why do we bow our heads at the name of Jesus?

A time-honored custom of the Christian Church is to instruct the congregation at worship to bow their heads every time the name of Jesus is uttered during the Mass. A congregation well trained in this practice will be alert to listen for it especially during the Readings or Sermon, during which it is more difficult to expect the times when Jesus' name will be heard. The custom therefore provides a means of helping the congregation learn to pay attention to the words they hear. More than this, however, it is an expression of faith, which knows that the holy name of Jesus is the most blessed utterance in all creation, being the name of Him who has redeemed us from sin, death, and everlasting condemnation, and has brought us to Himself by His blood. Thus we revere and adore Him in this simple way—simple, as it is less liturgically profound than genuflexion—every time we hear His name, in accordance with the words of St. Paul, "at the name of Jesus every knee should bow" (Phil. 2:10). ✠

Why does the pastor hold his fingers a certain way when he blesses the congregation?

When giving a blessing or benediction, the pastor's fingers may be held in a way which approximates certain letters which abbreviate *Jesus Christ*. The pastor's index finger is held straight up, approximating the Greek *I*; his second finger is curved, for the Greek *C*; his third finger is crossed with his thumb, for the Greek *X*: and his fourth finger is curved, for another Greek *C*. This therefore makes four Greek letters: *ICXC*. These letters are often seen on icons as two words: *IC XC*. In the early Greek Bibles, a common way of abbreviating an often-used word was to write only the first and last letter of the word, with a line above the abbreviation. Thus, IC abbreviates *IECOUC*, or actually *IESOUS*, since the Greek C was an early form of S. In English, of course, it's *JESUS*. The Greek *XC* abbreviates *XPICTOC*, which is *CHRISTOS*, or in English, *CHRIST*. In short, *ICXC* is *IC XC*, which means JESUS CHRIST. Thus, the pastoral benedictions are made with the sign of the cross, while the fingers designate the One who was crucified on the cross, namely JESUS CHRIST. The blessing is therefore made with a visible sign that it is Jesus Christ the Crucified who is the source and cause of the blessing given. ✠

THE LUTHERAN MASS, BY PARTS

Why do we make the sign of the cross?

The making of the sign of the holy cross is perhaps the oldest rubric in the history of the Christian Church, likely dating to the times of the apostles themselves. It is good to know this, inasmuch as there are those who are reluctant to make the sign on themselves, calling it "Catholic." Indeed it is catholic, that is, in the best tradition of the holy Christian Church of all time (for that is what catholic really means; the term is more than a designation for a certain church body).

The sign of the cross is made with the right hand, fingers touching first the forehead, then the breastbone, then right shoulder, then left, and finally both hands coming together in the posture of prayer. This is actually the reverse of the way the sign is made in the Anglican and Roman Catholic churches; Lutherans make the sign, rather, in the same manner as the Eastern Orthodox (right to left, rather than left to right). The reason for this is that we consider the making of the sign of the cross on ourselves as a response of faith to the activity of God among us. The sign of the holy cross was made first by the pastor (in the stead of Christ) on the recipient of Holy Baptism, with the words: "Receive the sign of the holy cross, both upon the forehead and upon the heart, in token that you have been redeemed by Christ the Crucified." In Baptism, Christ the Crucified is given to the one being baptized; the giving and receiving of the sign of the cross is a token of this truth. Since the pastor makes the sign with his right hand, he signs toward his own right, which on the recipient is a movement from his right to his left across the heart. From Baptism, faith begins to respond: the new creature born at the font is perpetually returning thereto, in prayer and supplication, with thanksgiving. Thus it is most appropriate for the faithful, who have been baptized, to begin making the sign of the cross upon themselves, in effect retracing the sign first made upon them in Baptism. The retracing of the cross moves across the same lines the pastor made; hence, from top to bottom, and then from right to left.

During the Mass, there are several opportunities for making the sign of the cross. These are most easily discerned by paying attention to the times the pastor signs the congregation. At these times it is good also to sign oneself. Also, it is appropriate at the Invocation, which is a repetition of the baptismal formula, at the close of the Our

Father and of the Creed, and indeed, whenever the Trinitarian name is uttered. It is also proper just before receiving each kind in the Sacrament: this is a way of saying to oneself, I need not fear unworthy reception of these Holy Things, knowing that in Baptism I am washed in Christ whom I also receive here.

The sign of the holy cross, when it is accompanied by faith, is a most powerful weapon for the faithful. Indeed, St. Paul exhorts the Ephesians to take the breastplate of righteousness, which we might consider his own way of saying, as Luther also does in the Small Catechism, Make the sign of the holy cross. ✠

Why does the Sunday Mass always open with confession of sins and absolution? And what is the difference between corporate and private confession and absolution?

Actually, the Mass doesn't "open" until *after* the confession and absolution. The corporate confession and the absolution then given by the pastor are preparatory to the Mass itself, which opens after the absolution, with the Introit. Corporate confession, whose technical term is the *confiteor* (Latin for "I confess"), is usually introduced by an opening hymn of invocation, which calls upon God, and then the Invocation itself ("In the name of the Father," etc.). This *corporate* confession and absolution is actually an adaptation of *individual* confession and absolution, which at one time was the norm. Christian people would routinely go to the church to confess their sins *privately* before the pastor, and receive private absolution. This practice has sometimes been called "the forgotten Sacrament" because it fell into disuse in much of Lutheranism. Though corporate confession to some degree replaced it, corporate confession does not provide an opportunity for the penitent sinner to confess in particular those sins which have been grieving to his conscience, as the Catechism teaches. The Catechism speaks highly of this blessed gift, for its abiding comfort for the Christian and his tormented conscience. In recent years there have been attempts to recover the practice of private confession. Some newer hymnals provide brief liturgical formats for individual (or private) confession. ✠

Why does the pastor walk toward the altar during the singing of the Introit?

The word *Introit* means "entrance," and is the point at which we enter into the Mass. (The opening hymn and the confession and absolution, which precede the Introit, are preparatory to the Mass, but are not in fact part of the Mass itself.) The service opens with the Introit because here the faithful of God enter by faith into His holy place. This is signified by the movement which the celebrant makes toward the altar while the Introit is sung. The celebrant is the representative of Christ among us, which is why he might appropriately be vested in a chasuble, and since we are all *in Christ*, as St. Paul says, therefore we are all, iconically speaking, "in the celebrant," who thus acts not only in the stead of Christ, but in the stead of Christ's Body, the Church. Therefore when the celebrant approaches the altar, in truth *all* are approaching the altar. This is a priestly function of the Holy Ministry. The movement is made by one man, but it is a movement of the whole Church. This is fitting, because it serves to remind us that the whole Church is one, united in the one man Jesus Christ. It is also appropriate, therefore, for everyone to make the sign of the holy cross as the celebrant enters the holy place (the chancel), or even, as is the custom of some, to make the sign three times: once, as the celebrant begins his walk, again, as he passes into the chancel, and again, as he arrives, genuflects, and kisses the altar. This is in token that it is because of our baptismal faith that we stand united in one Christ, and enter with Him into the presence of His Father, as signified by the entrance of the celebrant. ✠

Why do we sing "Lord, have mercy" right after the Introit?

The words "Lord, have mercy" are a translation of the Greek *Kyrie eleison*, which is why this part of the Mass is called "the Kyrie" (pronounced *kee-ree-yay*). Since the Introit is the "entrance," wherein we all enter by faith into the presence of the living God, it is most appropriate for us to utter these words at once: "Lord, have mercy!" If even people as pious as Isaiah (cf. Isa. 6:5) or St. Peter (cf. St. Luke 5:8) find themselves woefully and miserably out of place in the presence of the holy God, certainly it is right for us to see ourselves in this way, upon first entering into His sacred presence in the Mass. But we also rightly cry at once for mercy, using the very same words as blind Bartimaeus, the ten lepers, and others who were brought to Jesus. We cry for mercy in the sure confidence that we shall receive it, for God is merciful and kind to His people. Our crying out for mercy *immediately* upon entering the holy place by faith indicates our awareness both of our own unrighteousness, and of the righteousness which He freely gives to us who claim no merit of our own. ✠

Why do we sing the Gloria right after the Kyrie?

During the Mass, we sing "Lord, have mercy" immediately after the Introit, that is, as soon as the pastor has approached the altar for the first time. On Sundays outside of penitential times, the Church has traditionally augmented the Kyrie with the Gloria in Excelsis, which is also called the Greater Gloria. (Traditionally this Gloria is not sung at weekday Masses unless they are feasts of the first class or feasts of our Lord). This approach is to signify the approach of faith, as the writer to the Hebrews says, "Draw near to God." As soon as we enter the holy place we cry out for mercy, thereby acknowledging our dire need for mercy in the presence of the holy God. Yet we also know that this God is indeed a merciful God. We do not pray as if to make God merciful by our petitions. Rather, we know He is so. Therefore as soon as we have cried out for mercy, we at once express our confidence in this mercy by singing the song of the angels at the birth of Christ: "Glory to God in the highest, and peace on earth, goodwill toward men." With these words our hearts are again brought to Bethlehem and the One whose holy birth has joined heaven and earth. In Him is our confidence that we shall receive mercy. For He who is heavenly from all eternity is now also become earthly for all eternity, that we who are earthly might become heavenly in Him, for all eternity. Therein we find confidence that God shall indeed be merciful to us. ✠

Why does the Salutation precede the Collect?

Immediately before the Collect in the Mass, the pastor turns to face the people, and says, "The Lord be with you," to which they reply, "And with thy spirit." This, along with the Collect itself, is in preparation for the hearing of the reading of the Word of God. The pastor's words, "The Lord be with you," are an adaptation of the words of the risen Christ to His disciples, "Peace be with you." Some traditions retained the latter formula when spoken by a bishop. These words, which are the first words Christ said to the disciples when He appeared to them in the upper room, indicate the putting away of their sins, even as the Resurrection itself demonstrates this. When the pastor says the words of the Salutation, he is repeating the pattern set by Christ Himself. These are the first words he says to the people as pastor (since the preparatory service is not part of the Mass itself). As the first words from the mouth of Christ's ambassador to His people, they reestablish the fact that their forgiveness has been obtained by His resurrection and is therefore rightly granted at once.

When the people reply, "And with thy spirit," they are not merely responding in kind, but are praying for their pastor, that the Holy Spirit may rest upon him, for now he will speak to them as bearer of the office of the Holy Spirit. Therefore grace is required, that the pastor may be faithful in the carrying out of his duty, that is, that all of the words he speaks, including the words of the sermon, might be words fitly spoken as coming from God's ambassador to them. ✠

Why does the pastor say the Collect by himself?

After the Kyrie and Gloria are sung, the Collect is chanted. This is the prayer for the day, and is called a *collect* because it is the prayer of the collected faithful. It is prayed with one voice, by the pastor alone, to signify the unity of the faith. This is the prayer of the whole Church, collected into a unity. It is not only those *collected* in one particular church building that pray here, but the whole Christian Church. Even the saints triumphant pray with us here, are collected with us here. The pastor, chanting alone, is praying in the stead of the whole Church, with a single voice. Then, all respond with *Amen*, to indicate our agreement in unity of the Christian faith. ✠

Why do the Readings always include Epistle and Gospel, in that order?

As it was with the sacred Scriptures in Israel's day, so today there are two parts to the Scriptures of the New Testament. Then, there were Moses and the Prophets. Now, there are the Gospels and the Epistles. And yet, as the books of Moses (the first five books of the Bible, called the *Pentateuch*) were the foundation upon which the Prophets were laid, so also, the Gospels are the foundation upon which the Epistles are laid.

This is the reason the Gospels appear first in the New Testament, and it is also the reason the Gospel Reading is given last. In order of placement in the New Testament, the Gospels are given the most prominent position, that is, first, and in order of public reading they are also given the most prominent position, which in the case of oral utterance is last.

Moreover, it is also fitting that an Old Testament Reading regularly accompany these two Readings, to show that the New Testament arises out of the Old, and that all the sacred Scriptures are a unity. ✠

Why is the Bible carried from the right to the left side as one faces the altar for the reading of the Gospel?

During the Mass, there are ordinarily three Readings: the Old Testament, the Epistle, and the Gospel. All three are worthy of our special attention, of course, since they are words from the Sacred Scriptures, and therefore words of God. But of those, the Church has traditionally regarded the words from the Gospels as being the greatest, since the Gospels (St. Matthew, St. Mark, St. Luke, and St. John) are the accounts of Christ in the flesh and His holy ministry among us, and they contain also His very words. This is why all rise for the reading of the Gospel, even as the members of any assembly customarily rise for the entrance of a president, king, or other dignitary. Since we believe that through the Gospel Christ Himself comes and dwells with us, therefore it is fitting that we rise and sing *Alleluias* to acknowledge His entrance to sit in the midst of us when the Gospel is about to be read. Moreover, the Gospel is meant for all the world to hear; and therefore from ancient times there has been a movement of the reader toward the north, in the churches (which generally faced the east). For the heathen dwelt mostly to the north. This movement of the reader thus formed a vector of sorts, an arrow. By this ritual, then, an understanding obtains that this Gospel is for all, even the heathen "in the north." In the Mass, everything moves toward the "north": the lighting of the candles, the Bible, the Readings, the reader, even the altar book.

Sometimes, at higher feasts and festivals, the movement of the reader and Gospel book toward the "north" is highlighted also by a movement first into the nave, to stand directly in the midst of the congregation. This is to depict the coming of Christ into the flesh, to dwell among us. So let us with ready and willing feet rise alertly for the reading of the Gospel, and see the movement of the book and its reader as a holy illustration that the Gospel pertains to the incarnation of God, to dwell among us, and that it is meant for all the world to hear. ✠

Why is the Gradual inserted between the Readings?

The Gradual, which consists in the chanting of a psalm or part thereof, is so called because there was formerly a step, called the *gradine*, on which the reader stood to chant the psalm following the First Reading, or Epistle.

Traditionally there have been four parts of the Mass sung by the choir: Introit, Gradual, Offertory, and Communion. Unlike the other three, the Gradual did not arise from the desire or need to fill up the time during which something else was being done in the Mass, but is probably as old as the Readings themselves. The idea of interspersing a psalm or psalms with the Readings appointed for the day is a practice carried over from the synagogue.

This insertion of a psalm between the Readings helps to provide a stream of faith's "language," a mind-set or "zone" of thought springing primarily from the Psalter, in the midst of which the Readings are heard. Introit, Psalm, and Sentence all serve this same purpose. The words of faith's language flow around and through the Readings, and indicate that the Word of God is itself living and active, like a river or stream. ✠

Why is the Triple Hallelujah sung before the Gospel?

The Hebrew word *Hallelujah* means "Praise God," and is carried into the Latin tongue without translation as *Alleluia*. Its use in the medieval Roman Church was restricted to Eastertide, as an expression of the Church's highest joy. It was sung with long *melismata* or *neumes* (long musical phrases on a single syllable), as an expression of joy too deep for words, the joy of the resurrection of Christ.

Our use of the Triple Hallelujah before the Gospel is a related use, since we know that our hearing of the words of Christ in the Gospel is nothing less than a hearing of the Resurrected One speaking among us. Such knowledge gives abiding joy, and thus it is fitting to rise in anticipation of the Gospel and to sing *Hallelujahs*.

In the Western Church we omit the *Hallelujahs* from Septuagesima until Easter as an aural fast. There is even an ancient hymn for Septuagesima which bids farewell to the Hallelujah. This serves to make the anticipation for Easter, and the joy of Easter, all the greater. The joy of Christ's resurrection can scarcely be better expressed than by simple *Hallelujahs*. ✠

Why does the Triple Hallelujah have a sentence attached to it?

This sentence is actually called a "Sentence for the Season" and is appended to the Triple Hallelujah as a further preparation for the reading of the Gospel. It is seasonal, which means that its content changes as the seasons of the liturgical calendar change. Its content is also generally a clear reflection of the season in which it is found. This prepares the hearers by implicitly reminding them that the Gospel is tied to the year, and the year to their lives, and their lives to God, who is Himself the "Ancient of Days." During the penitential season leading to Easter, the Sentence stands alone, since *Hallelujahs* are omitted. ✠

Why do we confess the Creed after hearing the Gospel?

During the Sunday Mass, the Nicene Creed is confessed after the Gospel has been heard. Thus we express our belief that the Christian faith which we confess is given *by* the Gospel we have heard.

In some settings of the Mass, the Creed is confessed before the Sermon, and in others, it comes after the Sermon. In the former case, where the Creed comes before the Sermon, we express the conviction that the Sermon should be rooted in the Gospel as we have confessed it, and that it should not deviate from this faith. In the latter case, however, where the Creed comes after the Sermon, this former conviction is simply *assumed* to be the case, which, by some reckoning, actually makes the conviction a stronger one. At the same time another conviction is implied, namely, that the Gospel when it is preached is as much the Gospel as when it is heard in the Readings. In either case, to confess the Creed immediately upon hearing the Word is to imply that faith comes by hearing, that is, to acknowledge the power of the Word to create the faith we confess.

According to traditional rubrics, the Creed is said during all feasts of the first class, feasts of our Lord, and Sunday feasts, but is omitted during any other weekday Masses. This serves to elevate the status of the feasts. ✠

Why is the Sermon preached from the pulpit?

The pulpit and lectern may be seen as embellishments of two of the horns, or corners, of the altar, the traditional places from which the Word of God sounds forth. In Old Testament temple worship the four horns of a freestanding altar were actually projections, to which the sacrificial lamb was bound. As the sacrifice was bound to the horns of the altar (Ps. 118:27), so today, in the age of fulfillment, the Word of God is the message of Christ crucified, our sacrificial Lamb.

Traditions are divided regarding the placement of the pulpit, some placing it at the Gospel side (the left horn, from which the Gospel is read), and others at the Epistle side (the right horn, from which the Epistle is read). The former placement highlights the importance of the Sermon's content, that being primarily exposition of the Gospel Reading, and by extension also proclamation of the Gospel in all its fullness, and to all the world. The latter placement, on the Epistle side, highlights rather the importance of the Sermon's addressees, namely, the congregation. As the Epistles were directed specifically to the Church, so the Sermon is directed to the Church. ✠

Why is the offering collected when it is?

During the Mass, the collection of the offerings takes place while the altar is being prepared for Holy Communion. There is an important connection here between the elements used (the bread and the wine) and the offerings collected. In the early church, the Offertory was a time of movement in the liturgy: it was sung while the bread and wine were brought forth from the congregation as elements being offered to God for use in the Sacrament. According to some traditions, the bread and wine themselves are brought forward by the congregation. In others, they are brought to the altar by a server or subdeacon. By extension, the offerings of money are collected while the altar is being prepared, for the money collected is used to provide for the elements, the altar, the building, the pastor, and indeed everything we need here.

Behold now what Christ does with these offerings: He receives them, and then, by His Word, gives them back to us as His Body and Blood. Here is the great mystery of the altar, that God's pure grace is operative here, as He takes what we offer Him, feeble, poor, and by no means sufficient to merit any good from Him, and gives it back to us as His own life-giving food. This is just like the great mystery of the Incarnation, wherein Christ received the poor, feeble flesh that the Blessed Virgin gave Him, and united it with His majestic divinity to give us life and salvation. ✠

Why is the General Prayer positioned after the Sermon and before the Administration of the Sacrament?

The General Prayer, also called The Prayer of the Church, is a gathering point for the Christian Church as it prepares to partake in the Blessed Sacrament. In ancient times, the names of people for whom prayers were intended were written on cards called *diptychs*, and while prayers were offered for the conversion of the heathen, only the names of Christians appeared on the *diptychs*. Although this custom does not survive, still the idea is rightly to be preserved that here the members of the church are praying for one another, and so bearing one another's burdens. This unifying prayer thus serves as a key preparation for attending together at the altar.

In some traditions, the kiss of peace still remains from the ancient church as a further gesture of unity. In any case, there must be no divisions among Christians who commune together. ✠

Why is the altar in the middle?

Churches vary greatly in architectural style, and the style of the interior is generally somewhat representative of what that church believes. Some churches have a very prominent pulpit, elevated above everything else and planted right in the center. This no doubt is meant to proclaim that the preaching of the Word of God is of primary importance. Indeed, Lutheran churches have historically had *extremely* high pulpits, requiring many steps for the preacher to ascend.

Yet in Lutheran churches it is also generally true—as is the case in many other traditional churches—that the pulpit, high and prominent as it may be, is not in the center. Rather, it is off to one side, and the altar stands alone in the center. This sends a strong visual message: the preaching of the sermon, as important and sacred a thing as it is, is not as central to the Church's life as the Holy Sacrament of the Altar. For the sermon *preaches* Christ, but the Sacrament *is* Christ, as He said, "This is My Body." Therefore the pulpit is appropriately placed to one side, that the preacher may refer to that which is central, namely, Christ; and the altar is appropriately placed in the center, while the Sacrament is appropriately placed on the center of the altar. This puts Christ in the center of our churches, of our worship, and of our lives. ✠

Why do we bow or kneel to the altar?

Jesus once said to the Pharisees that the gold of the temple is sanctified by the temple. So the holiness of the temple dictated that those things pertaining to it were also holy.

Jesus also said, referring to Himself, "One greater than the temple is here." Now if Jesus' holiness is greater than the holiness of the temple, surely those things pertaining to Jesus Himself are also holy.

In the Holy Supper Christ Himself is truly present, for He said, "This is My Body." Therefore, according to His own words, it is His true Body which sits on the paten (the plate) which sits on the altar. For the bread is as much Christ's Body as His Body on the cross. Since this is so, it is surely appropriate to give highest reverence to His Body there, according to this faith. Therefore the people of God rightly bend the knee, to honor and adore Him where He is truly found.

Not only do we reverence the Sacrament sitting on the altar, however. Since the temple sanctifies the gold, so also the Body of Christ sanctifies the altar. We call the altar *holy* because it is the place from which Christ's Body is given.

Therefore when the Sacrament is on the altar, we kneel (which is more profound than bowing) when we come to the altar to receive the Sacrament; but even when the Sacrament is not there, we bow, whenever we pass the altar.

It is also appropriate to observe this custom before entering or upon leaving the pew: when the Sacrament is present, to kneel and make the sign of the cross; or when the Sacrament is not present, to bow. There is also a venerable custom of bowing and making the sign of the cross upon entering or leaving the church.

This is a small way of being reminded either that Christ's holy Body is present or has sanctified the altar which pertains to it. How very blessed it is to know this when we receive Christ's Body and His Blood in the Supper. For thereby we ourselves are sanctified (and saved!), as our most holy faith confesses. ✠

Why do we sometimes kneel and sometimes only bow toward the altar?

The centrality of the altar in our churches is a vivid reminder of the centrality of the Holy Sacrament of Christ's Body and Blood in the Mass, since the Sacrament is placed on the altar. Here—as we believe, teach, and confess—is where Christ is found. He sits on the altar! And even when the Sacrament isn't there, since the altar is His throne, we reverence.

Historically and traditionally, there has been a difference in the way people would reverence the altar, depending on whether the Sacrament was actually on the altar or not. If the altar did not have the Sacrament on it, the people simply bowed toward it; but if they could see that the Sacrament was there, they knelt, even on entering the church. This reflected the belief that even elements reserved from a prior celebration of the Sacrament still are in fact what Christ has called them, His Body and Blood.

People are generally aware that in some churches—most notably Roman Catholic—people genuflect (drop to one knee) before entering the pew. What is perhaps less well known is the origin of this practice: it always had to do with whether the Sacrament was on the altar. Since in some churches the Sacrament is *always* on or near the altar, the people simply genuflected all the time. It wasn't simply a thing to do on entering their pew; it was a reverence toward the Sacrament. The historic rule of thumb—which has largely been forgotten in our day—was that whether one genuflected or merely bowed was determined by whether the consecrated elements of the Sacrament were there or not.

Lutherans have known some different ways of reverencing: among some, it is customary to enter one's pew and to stand and pray toward the altar before sitting. Others bow upon entering the pew. Some do genuflect, if the Sacrament is present. The great majority of Lutherans have customarily done their most profound genuflecting at the altar, when they receive the Sacrament. There they do a double genuflexion (they kneel with *both* knees).

It is important that our practice be informed by our theology. What we believe ought to affect what we do; thus kneeling is always appropriate if Christ's Body and Blood are present. This is especially so in view of the fact that there have been churches who do not believe that the Sacrament truly is Christ, so they *refuse* to kneel. How much more ought we confess with our knees, then. For we believe Christ's words: "This is My Body; this is My Blood." ✠

THE ADMINISTRATION OF THE BLESSED SACRAMENT, BY PARTS

Why does the celebrant say "Lift up your hearts" while lifting his hands during the Preface?

During the Mass, the Preface comes after the Prayer of the Church, when we begin to turn our attention directly to the Sacrament of the Altar. The celebrant first says, "The Lord be with you," because it is a prayer that the Lord would be merciful in granting His people the faith needed to benefit from this great feast of the Lord's Body and Blood. Then he says, "Lift up your hearts," and the people respond, "We lift them up unto the Lord." This is based on Lamentations 3:41-42: "Let us lift our hearts and hands to God in heaven. We have transgressed and rebelled." So the lifting up that takes place, both of the hearts and of the hands (as the celebrant lifts his hands at this point), is in effect an acknowledgment that we have transgressed; we need to be cleansed of our sins. How fitting, therefore, that we should repeat these words prior to our reception of the Sacrament, by which we are cleansed and forgiven. Since we know that this is about to happen, we say immediately following, also during the Preface: "Let us give thanks unto the Lord, our God. It is meet and right so to do." ✠

Why does the Sanctus blend two separate parts of Scripture?

The Sanctus, so named because it is Latin for "Holy," as in "Holy, holy, holy, Lord God of Sabaoth," appropriately precedes the words of Christ's institution of the Sacrament, precisely because it serves to blend two parts and themes of Scripture together.

The first part is the vision of Isaiah, in which the seraphim cry "Holy, holy, holy" to one another, smoke arises, the lintels shake, and the prophet is overawed in his confrontation with the majesty of the Triune God. So ought we to be overawed by an awareness that we here are in the presence of Almighty God.

The second part is from the procession of Palm Sunday, when the children joyously cry out "Hosanna" to Christ, who rides a donkey into Jerusalem to do the work of our salvation. So ought we joyously cry, for in the Supper Christ comes to us to save us.

The blending of these two disjunct passages provides a poignant reminder to us that at the altar the majesty of Almighty God is bound to the Sacrament, which is given for us and for our salvation. ✠

Why does the pastor hold his hands up high over his head for the Lord's Prayer?

Following the Preface at Mass, the pastor turns to the altar and intones the Proper Preface, that is, the "seasonal" preface in preparation for the Supper. Following this in some traditions is an *epiclesis*, or prayer for the Holy Spirit, and then, as the highest of these consecutive prayers, the "Our Father," which is the Lord's Prayer. Traditions which employ the epiclesis generally have the Our Father after the Words of Institution are spoken. Traditions which do not employ the epiclesis generally have the Our Father before the Verba, in which case, the Our Father serves as the epiclesis, which calls upon God for His blessing. This prayer is not only the highest of the prayers at Mass, but of all prayers, since it is the prayer our Lord Jesus Himself taught us to pray. Therefore it is most fitting that, in recognition of this, the celebrant should extend his hands higher than he had been extending them for the other prayers. The extension and raising of the hands is the ancient posture of prayer, and normally during Mass the pastor so prays. To distinguish the Our Father alone above all the others, here he raises his hands higher. For no other prayer in the service does he raise his hands this high; it is therefore a subtle reminder of the fact that when we pray the Our Father, we are praying the very best prayer we could possibly pray. ✠

Why does the pastor alone say the Lord's Prayer sometimes?

The Lord's Prayer (the "Our Father") is the most excellent of all prayers, being so called because the Lord Jesus gave it to us Himself, and told His disciples to pray saying precisely these words ("When you pray, say: Our Father," etc.). Therefore it ought to be first on the lips of every Christian, day and night. In addition to this, an ancient and venerable custom elevates its significance during the Mass, by providing the rubric that has the celebrant alone chanting or saying these words aloud, while the congregation prays them silently. This distinguishes the Mass from the prayer offices of Matins and Vespers, which have the congregation saying all the words of the Lord's Prayer together.

The custom provides a special adornment for this prayer at a time when it is used in connection with the Sacrament, a connection which can be discerned quickly by virtue of the celebrant's chanting or saying also the Verba (the Words of Institution) in immediate proximity, either following or preceding. By this practice, the Our Father is seen as the central, and indeed only indispensable, ingredient in the canon of the Mass, that prayer of the celebrant which from antiquity was woven together with the Verba.

Both the Our Father and the Verba come from Christ Himself, with His expressed intention that they be repeated (in the case of the Sacrament, this intention is expressed by the words "This do"). They thus stand side by side as the most distinguished words in the entire service, with the implied message that the petitions of the Our Father are *answered* by the Sacrament. Herein is the heart of our faith expressed. ✠

Why does the celebrant look up during a part of the Words of Institution?

During the Mass, when the Words of Institution (also called the *Verba*) are repeated, the celebrant engages in certain actions, in repetition of the actions of our Lord in His institution of the Supper. During the words "took bread," he *takes* the bread, and during the words "and when He had given thanks," he looks up in thanksgiving. This looking up is the ancient gesture of thanksgiving, which we see in Jesus Himself. St. Matthew (14:15-21, the feeding of the five thousand) records that "looking up to heaven, He blessed and broke and gave the loaves." By "looking up to heaven" while "blessing" (that is, giving thanks) He means to acknowledge the source of the bread, and of every good gift. St. James also indicates this truth, saying, "Every good gift and every perfect gift is from above, and comes down from the Father of lights" (James 1:17).

The Roman liturgy goes so far as actually to say that Jesus "looked up" as He gave thanks at the Supper, but the Lutheran Church's version is a verbatim (word-for-word) conflation of the Eucharistic texts. It is nevertheless safe to assume that Jesus did in fact look up at this point, in accordance with His custom.

When the celebrant repeats the gesture of Jesus during the consecration of the elements, especially the words "when He had given thanks," he gives a visual reminder that here he is actually standing in for Jesus, in His stead, and by His command. We are not merely "acting out" the scene here; rather the *very same Supper* is being continued here. We may know that here, through the ministry of His humble servant, truly Jesus Himself is the One who is active, giving to us again His own Body and Blood, just as He once gave it to His twelve disciples. ✠

Why in the chanting of the Words of Institution are the words of Christ on a lower note?

The traditional chant tones for the Words of Institution use lower tones for the words of Christ. This principle was also used in Reformation times for the chanting of the Gospels themselves, which was customary. Whenever the words of Christ were said, a lower tone was used. This was the traditional way of giving a higher honor to the words of the Incarnate One. It is for the same reason, to show a higher honor, that we stand for the reading of the Gospel. The use of lower tones suggests a greater solemnity, and thus provides the ear with a cue that these words are the most significant of all. Indeed, when the words of Christ are heard, they are heard as though Christ Himself were speaking them. The reason the words of our faith are chanted at all is to indicate their holy character. We provide for their oral repetition the best kind of sound of which we are capable, namely, the sound of singing. ✠

Why are the Host and cup elevated at the Lord's Supper?

The following is written by the Reverend Michael James Hill, of Milwaukee, Wisconsin.

Martin Luther wrote of the elevation (raising) of the elements at the Lord's Supper in his introduction to the *Deutsche Messe* (German Mass), 1526: "We do not want to abolish the elevation, but retain it because it goes well with the German Sanctus and signifies that Christ has commanded us to remember him." The German Sanctus that Luther refers to has been translated and appears in our English hymnals as "Isaiah, Mighty Seer." The words of Luther's Sanctus show us that our ordinary Sanctus ("Holy, holy, holy") is drawn from Isaiah 6:1–7.

Isaiah 6 begins: "In the year that King Uzziah died, I saw the Lord sitting on a throne, high and lifted up, and the train of His robe filled the temple."

At the Words of Institution we sing, "Holy, holy, holy, Lord God of Sabaoth," even as the angels sang when Isaiah saw the Lord in the temple. Our Lord has promised us that where His Word is given with bread and wine, there is His Body and Blood, given and shed for the forgiveness of sins. As we believe in the real presence of Christ hidden under the Sacrament, so we show reverence to the Lord.

The elevation of the elements is therefore in keeping with other common practices Lutherans have long done at the Lord's altar: kneeling as one approaches to commune, bowing and/or making the sign of the cross at the dismissal of the table. All of these practices are neither forbidden nor commanded by God, but in Christian freedom we adopted them to remind ourselves that this is no ordinary meal. The Lord has entered His temple. ✠

Why does the celebrant elevate Host and cup after each is consecrated?

At this point in the Mass we have reached the heart of our Christian faith: we affirm with this elevation that here is where Christ is to be found: "This is My Body," said He; and therefore we believe that this consecrated Host is truly His Body; so likewise with the cup. While many deny the possibility of this, since it does not sound very reasonable at all, we not only affirm it, but we affirm it with all boldness. The elevation of the elements is therefore an unspoken statement of faith. We wouldn't elevate mere symbols, after all; we wouldn't hold high for adoration and worship some earthly, corruptible thing, as a mere piece of bread would be. Certainly not, for that would be blasphemy! Let anyone who denies the real presence in the Sacrament come and accuse us of blasphemy, then, for if he does, then we will know that by elevating the elements we are doing the right thing! Should not our faith be offensive to such a one, seeing how offensive likewise it is to us to say these elements are anything less than what Christ Himself said they were? For what could truly be more blasphemous than to declare that these are *not* His Body and His Blood? He is the One who said they were. How, then, might we show that we affirm what He Himself has said? Surely, elevation of the elements is in order. And the people, seeing the elements elevated so, will surely do well to bow or genuflect in reverence toward the holy Body and Blood of Christ. For Christ Himself has said it. ✠

Why does the pastor hold aloft the Host and cup and face the people for the Pax Domini, following the Words of Institution?

Immediately after the Words of Institution, the celebrant turns to face the people, holding the chalice aloft in his left hand and the Host above it, while saying, "The peace of the Lord be with you always." This is because of the words of the risen Christ to His disciples, "Peace be with you."

These words indicate the putting away of their sins, even as the Resurrection itself demonstrates this. When the celebrant repeats these words here, while holding the elements of the Sacrament aloft, he is making a clear connection between the eternal peace of Christ, won for us by His bodily crucifixion and the shedding of His Blood, and this very same Body and Blood, given to us here in the Sacrament. ✠

Why does the celebrant say, after the Words of Institution, "Behold the Lamb of God who takes away the sin of the world," while holding high the elements?

This practice was taught by the Reverend Wilhelm Loehe, the German pastor who supplied the early Missouri Synod with its first pastors in the mid-nineteenth century. The practice has from antiquity been a traditional part of the

Western rite, said in connection with the Agnus Dei ("O Christ, Thou Lamb of God," etc.). The high point of the Mass having just been reached with the recitation of the Words of Institution, it is most fitting for the celebrant now to do exactly as John the Baptist did. Recall how John had said these same words when he saw Jesus coming to him (St. John 1:29). Here, in the Sacrament, is the same Christ. It is proper, then, for all the congregation to utter a robust Amen in response, as well as to sing the Agnus Dei. ✠

Why does the pastor kneel during the singing of the Agnus Dei?

After the Words of Institution have been spoken, the celebrant turns and holds Host and cup before the people, declaring, "Behold the Lamb of God who takes away the sin of the world," to which the people respond with the traditional response of ancient Israel, "Amen!" Next, the people sing the Agnus Dei ("Lamb of God"), in preparation for reception of the Lamb of God in the Sacrament.

Meanwhile, the pastor is kneeling at the altar. This is the traditional posture of the celebrant for the Agnus Dei, during which he prays the *secreta*, which is the "private" prayer of preparation for his own reception of the Sacrament. In this the celebrant mimics and portrays Jesus, who in Gethsemane withdrew from His disciples a stone's throw away (St. Luke 22:41), to pray privately. Here again the distinction between celebrant and Christ is blurred, as the iconic nature of the office becomes manifest. The pastor will commune immediately after the Agnus Dei, since the celebrant always communes first and then feeds the people.

The traditional *secreta* includes the following: "I will receive the bread of thanksgiving and call upon the name of the Lord. Lord, I am not worthy that Thou shouldst come under my roof. Only say the word and my soul shall be healed" (cf. Ps. 116:17, St. Matt. 8:8).

Another appropriate form of the prayer of preparation is St. Bonaventure's thirteenth-century *Prayer of Humble Access*—appropriate, in fact, for anyone to pray before receiving the Sacrament—which runs as follows:

O Lord, who art Thou, and who am I, that I should presume to place Thee in the foul sewer of my body and soul. A thousand years of tears would not suffice for once worthily receiving so noble a Sacrament. How much more am I unworthy, wretched man, who daily sin, continue without amendment, and approach in sin. Yet Thy mercy is infinitely greater than my misery. Therefore, trusting in Thy mercy, I presume to approach. ✠

Why is the Sacrament something we eat and drink?

The first answer to that question has to be the simplest one: we eat and drink the Holy Supper because Jesus told us to do so. He said, "Take, eat," and, "Drink of it, all of you." And again, "This do." Therefore without question Christians learn to do this as a central ingredient of their most holy faith. No one can be forced, certainly; neither can one be forced to be a Christian. Christians learn to do what Christ wants them to do, especially in their worship of Him.

Secondly, as the ancient fathers have taught us well, it was by eating that sin entered into the world, so it is most fitting that by eating salvation should be given. The first eating brought death, the second brings life. The first eating was sinful, the second eating is for the forgiveness of sins.

Sacrament means "mystery." We participate in the mystery of God here, and partake in His eternal feast of salvation. Our participation is by eating and drinking because it is a feast.

It can also be said that eating and drinking are very simple things, very down-to-earth things. Therefore God in this way demonstrates His simple desire to have us know in no uncertain terms that our sins are forgiven. As surely as we eat and drink this, knowing it to be Christ's Body and Blood, so confident may we be that our sins are forgiven. ✠

Why do we come to the altar to commune?

In churches of the Reformed or Baptist tradition, one commonly finds communicants staying in their pews as the trays are passed down the line, in much the same fashion as the offering plates. Communicants take a piece of bread, and hold it until all have received theirs, and then when the minister says, "Take, eat," all eat at the same time. Then comes the tray containing cups of wine (or grape juice!), after which the tray is passed again, to receive the empty cups.

In Lutheran churches, by contrast, communicants come forward to receive at the altar, as is also the case among Roman Catholics, Eastern Orthodox, and Anglicans or Episcopalians. Why?

This custom reflects our understanding of our participation in the Sacrament, that it is not a symbolic gesture. It *truly* is Christ, and therefore we, according to ancient custom, receive Him with the reverence that befits this faith.

Interestingly, many (though not all) of the churches who have the practice of staying in the pews for Communion also have the custom of "altar calls." Altar calls are invitations to come forward and "accept Christ" into one's life. But those who come forward receive nothing. They might get "slain in the Spirit," falling down as if in a trance, or, in the less emotion-driven settings, they might simply stand at the front while prayer is said. They might get a hug.

What a telling comparison: in the latter case, people come forward to *give* their lives to Jesus, while in the former, they come forward to *receive* their lives *from* Jesus—for in the Sacrament we receive the forgiveness of sins, where, according to the Catechism, "there is also life and salvation." Here is a stark contrast between what essentially amounts, on the one hand, to doing something (accepting Christ) to "get saved," and on the other, doing something (coming forward for the Sacrament) because of what you already believe, namely, that Christ is giving Himself to you there. ✠

Why do we sing hymns during the Distribution?

It is fitting that the faithful who gather to await the coming of the Lord should sing: as St. Paul says, "Let the word of Christ dwell in you richly in all wisdom, teaching and admonishing one another in psalms and hymns and spiritual songs, singing with grace in your hearts to the Lord" (Col. 3:16). Gladness is universally expressed by singing, and therefore it is right that the faithful who gather for the Holy Sacrament (wherein the Lord comes to us) should also sing. The Apostolic Church did so, as it is written, "They ate their food with gladness and simplicity of heart, praising God" (Acts 2:47). St. Augustine says, "To sing belongs to lovers," and we, as lovers of God in the Holy Feast, rightly sing to Him in connection with our reception of Him. ✠

Why do we sing "Lord, now lettest Thou Thy servant depart in peace" after communing?

This post-Communion canticle, called the *Nunc Dimittis* (Latin for "now dismiss," the opening words of the canticle), is also called the Song of Simeon, for it is his response to receiving the Christ Child in his arms (St. Luke 2:25-32). For it had been revealed to him by the Holy Ghost that he, though we assume him to have been advanced in years, should not see death before he had seen the Lord's Christ. Thus when he at last sees the Child, with the words "My eyes have seen Your salvation" he is in effect saying, Now I can die in peace. Likewise we Christians, when we receive this same Christ at the altar, appropriately say the same thing as he. For we do not see the flesh of His Body, but we do see His Body all the same, for this bread is, as the Apostle says, the Communion of the Body of Christ, which means that the bread and Christ's Body have communed together and become one substance. Thus, beholding the bread, we behold Christ's Body; for they are the same thing. And we do not take Him into our arms, but receive Him by mouth, for He said, "Take, eat; this is My Body." Hence we, in as authentic a way as did Simeon, behold and receive Christ at the altar, and so we, according to the same faith as he expressed, say the same words, in effect meaning, Now I can die in peace. That is, now I can face anything and everything which the world, the flesh, and the devil may cast in my path, for my eyes have seen God's salvation; I have received my Christ here. ✠

Why do we sing responsively the Thanksgiving after the Nunc Dimittis?

The responsive singing of "Oh, give thanks unto the Lord, for He is good," with "And His mercy endureth forever," is the oldest responsorial liturgy extant, coming from the Psalms, especially Psalm 136, which employs the response "For His mercy endureth forever" at each verse. Its usage here, at the completion of the Distribution and Nunc Dimittis, is not only a fitting recapitulation of the goodness of God given in the Sacrament, but a liturgical mark and indication that all of the goodness and mercy of God may be found in the Sacrament, and even that every other reference to the goodness of God is fulfilled in the Sacrament. This is the final—the perpetually final—expression of thanks to God for His goodness, now that we have come to the pinnacle of everything that can rightly be called good. God not only made the world and called it good in the beginning, but now, in the end, joins Himself and His eternal goodness to us fallen creatures, to return to us for all eternity the dignity of His goodness. ✠

Why does the pastor, facing the people, raise his hands for the Benediction?

The Benediction (literally, "good words") comes from the blessing which Aaron have to the people in Numbers 6:24-26, and is sometimes referred to as the Aaronic Blessing. It employs the very same words, and as Aaron lifted his hands to bless the people, so does the celebrant.

Behind this is an understanding that Aaron was prefiguring Christ in His crucifixion, with arms outstretched. That is, the stretching out of Jesus' arms on the cross is the true cause and source of God's heavenly benediction.

So important is the Benediction that in some traditions, the congregation even kneels to receive it. It is the last summarizing statement of our most holy faith, expressing bodily both the crucifixion and blessing of Christ at once. He was crucified for you, so now He blesses you with an eternal benediction. ✠

OTHER SERVICES

Why does the pastor face sideways during some services?

A portable kneeler, also called the *prie-dieu*, may be used in services other than the Holy Communion service. This enables the pastor to conduct the prayer services without approaching the altar. Thus the altar is used only during the Mass. This serves to emphasize the importance of the Holy Sacrament. In Old Testament times, the high priest entered the Holy of Holies only when he brought the annual sacrifice on the Day of Atonement. So now in the Church, in New Testament times, the celebrant enters the chancel to celebrate the Sacrament. This is because the Sacrament is the fulfillment of all the Old Testament sacrifices, since it is the sacrificed Body of Christ and His holy Blood which was shed. These elements of His one-and-only sacrifice are what are given to the communicants who come forth. To reserve the altar and chancel for this purpose is to emphasize these truths. The use of the portable kneeler for the other services is helpful toward this end.

The positioning of the kneeler to face sideways is patterned after the churches and cathedrals in Europe whose "choir" sections also face sideways. The chapel at Concordia Theological Seminary, Fort Wayne, Indiana, also has a side-facing prie-dieu, used for Matins and Vespers. The use of such a kneeler is a very traditional practice, even if not as common in American churches.

More importantly, its purpose is to instruct. The pastor at prayer is doing two things at once: he is offering his prayers to God for himself and for the Church; and he is setting an example for his people to see. This too is biblical, for St. Paul also encouraged the Church to follow his example. Someone once said that seeing the pastor kneeling for prayer is like seeing Christ at prayer in Gethsemane; this is a helpful thought, since that pastor does well who presents Christ to the people in every part of his ministry. ✠

Why does the pastor wear a black "stole" for Matins and Vespers?

The black "stole" that a pastor may wear for Matins and Vespers is actually not a stole at all, but is called a tippet. The tippet designates the authority of the pastor to preach, but is not a Eucharistic vestment. That means it is not worn for Holy Communion. The stole, on the contrary, is a Eucharistic vestment, and actually is normally supposed to be worn beneath the chasuble, the long flowing poncho-like vestment worn by the celebrant at Holy Communion. This is why stoles come in the colors of the church year, while the tippet does not. Since the stole and chasuble go with the Sacrament, it is best to have them match the color of the altar from which the Sacrament is given. The tippet, on the other hand, is always black, simply designating the preaching office. Hence a tippet is not worn if Matins or Vespers are said or sung without a Sermon. In such cases, only cassock and surplice are to be worn (the black gown with the three-quarter-length white robe over the top). Thus, when at Matins or Vespers you see the pastor wearing the tippet, you know that you will soon be hearing him preach. ✠

Made in the USA
Lexington, KY
29 April 2012